A. I

KLOOOGS

...Curses of the Jews?...

Cover Design by
Johannes W. Bullmann
Edited by J. W. & D. Bullmann

ISBN 0-9714165-0-8

INSIGHTS FOR VACATING KLOOOGS

"BENJAMIN'S PURGATION'S OF THOUGHTS..."

EXORCISING THE MIND - RE-OPENING MANY UN-USED CIRCUITS OF THE BRAIN
SEARCHING INTO THE MEMORIES OF YOUR GENES
IS A MEANS TO AWAKENING INTELLIGENCE

YOURS...

The Klooogs often causing pain, in fact may not be yours directly - but may be locked in from a gene from some one else's past life's experience (memories in your genes)

GUILT IN THE UNIVERSAL HUMAN BRAIN

SURFACING THE KLOOOG TO VIEW ENDS THE CURSE...

Who am I you ask?
WHY, I am the best part of you...
The part you may have never met...

<u>Your life can be Klooogless...</u>
The Klooog Buster -A. Benjamin

CONTENTS

AUTHORS FOREWORD

Many of the ***Klooog*** stories were taken from some of my own life's experiences-others were drawn from knowledgeable reflections from others, the emotional connotations carefully held to the equations of the fact.

GETTING TO KNOW YOUR KLOOOGS:
Understanding why you get them could help save your life!

THE DEFINITION OF A KLOOOG:
A ***Klooog*** is often a nearly unbearable pain brought about at the most uninvited times in ones life perhaps by the revelation of some faded fantasy still fighting the present reality.

The heart and soul suddenly crying for the return of the fantasy; the mind needing to accept that it is over.

A ***Klooog*** is experienced when a person permits a thought to enter into his mind when one is least prepared.

The thought usually develops from a remembered occurrence that is now suddenly revealed as a negative past action, one that should not have occurred.

If the thought is precisely right, the chest may suddenly pain, and for short periods the heart seems to want to stop beating.

Sometimes it seems to stop sometimes it actually does; this is known as a ***Klooog***. It could be responsible at times to delivering a person to a depressed state of mind.

A critical time may approach when there is a desperate need to view and accept this reality.

You may find yourself connecting with many of the ***Klooog*** stories. Each ***Klooog*** story that the reader identifies with may in reality be the very same ***Klooog*** that has been previously responsible for some unremitting personal despair.

It is through the reading of this book and particularly through these ***Klooog*** stories that you may find the means to a welcome release.

It would give me great joy to know that you have.

RHYMES WITHOUT REASON - THE KLOOOG STORY

Thoughts from my youth return to times that riddle to confound me;
Too often do they reach to places stretched far beyond me.
Faded dreams awaken times that were good,
Loving parents gone to places that await me!
Remembering them, forgiving all that I could!
Feeling, knowing the things that I should,
Blindly they gave me what I could not see.
The heart forever searches this thought that tugs-
Crying, crying, ever to be free...
Free from these distorted Kloooogs!

PUPPY RECALLED

(To Hell with the Kloоog)

The man appeared to be headed straight to hell. He certainly had explicit and proper direction as to reach this objective. He was strongly advised not to stop for anything. His mouth was drooling and horns were already budding through the top of his head. His hands were sweaty cold. There seemed to be no stopping him. His heart was beating widely. A maniacal look of anticipation was on his face. Suddenly he became distracted for a moment. A small dog on the side of the road ignited an urge for him to stop. He pulled over, exited his vehicle and approached the little dog. The drizzle was beginning to turn to hard rain. The air was blowing cold and raw. He carefully and gently picked up the little dog and moved him a few feet off the road. The little dog was dying. He removed his warm sweater and covered the dog.

He sat on the ground with the dog for a long while until the Creator made his pickup. He left the little dog covered with his sweater and got back in his car. He became blinded by his tears. He had lost his dircctions; he was no longer headed for hell...The puppy was recalled.....

A KLOOOG THAT WAGS A TAIL

It was August of `74. My mind seemed to be elsewhere that cloudy gray afternoon, as I drove home from work perhaps a bit too fast. I was anxious to start my three day holiday. Suddenly a strange little dog decided to cross my path. Perhaps it was the drink I had before leaving work that prevented me from avoiding hitting that poor animal. I felt the car strike and heard the pitiful shriek of the little dog. I stopped the car and ran out. My heart was pounding. A little boy, perhaps no more than eight or nine, ran to the roadside where his dog now lay foundering. The dog tried to get up as the boy approached. I could see the little dogs tail begin to wag. The boy picked up the dog from the roadway, his tears now flowing freely. He carried his little dog toward his home. I followed in a fearful shock. I tried telling him how sorry I was. Not seeming to hear me, he pleadingly spoke to his little dog, "You'll be ok Pepper." The little dog tried just once to lick the boy's face as the child held him. He laid the dog to rest on his front porch. His tail suddenly stopped wagging. The boy then slowly looked up at me. All his words to me were in that long silent look. On a cloudy gray day sometimes, his looks come back to me and then it is gone. My Klooog is back.

SPRING: THE RETURN OF THE HORSE KLOOOG

It was 1976, the year that I joined the horse world. I loved, trusted, had faith, believed, and bled. I had hope. I fantasized. I gave and gave and gave. And sometimes, when Spring is suddenly upon me, I think of my horses no longer racing that I had failed. Perhaps they are lying on some supermarket shelf neatly packaged. It is then that I find myself once again viewing the position I had allowed myself to be led to. Had I dealt in reality, I would be training them for this next Spring meet. I often reflected how fortunate I am to have escaped so distorted a life as horse racing. I have accepted that this present perspective that has been delivered to me was a response to my desperate need to grasp reality. This view of reality will prevent me from ever returning to that wonderful world of heartbreaking fantasy. The magnificent smell of fresh hay and horse manure mixing with the early Spring air again excites me to re-invite these thoughts to fantasy. It is then I fester upon what a fool I had been, knowing that in all probability I still am. Suddenly, my thoughts seem to stop. I'm behind the sulky again, talking to my horse...my friend.

"You'll be all right, Sonny. Nice and easy."

I smile inside, enjoying my annual Spring horse Klooog.

MAX`S STORY

(The S.O.B. Klooog)

Max sits staring at the chessboard contemplating his next move.

"Jack, its your move! How about it? One of us is going to die before you move."

It was Jacks turn.

Jacks chess set is now mine.

I was hoping to leave him my chessboard, instead he left me his beautiful chess set.

They're all set up on my board. It seems that I must wait the coming eternity for him to move. It was only a game of chess, but how we did fight! I can't play again until our game is finished. Maybe I'll go to sleep soon to wake up and finish our last game- this Klooog is making me so damn tired-

"Jack, you son of a bitch, you could've at least waited and finished the game! I know you're waiting for me, you rusty old rat-no good screwball. Well, its my turn now, and I'm gonna take my sweet old ass time!

Jack...Jack you sonovabitch...I miss you.

THE OLD MAN KNOWS ITS NOT A KLOOOG

What if this pain in my left shoulder is nothing more than just re-telegraphing the pain over to my right foot, now a tugging from my mind, again trying to tell me that it is only the itch from my right cheek? All these are messages sent from my internal control center that I am now willed to ignore. How long can I remain safe? I seem not to care. These messages are constantly interfering with these rights to my wants. Nothing should interfere with that. What good are all these feelings from words for absolution when no one seems to equate-to care? I need to be alone again. Am I so different? Only on that island of perfection is to be God. It is not my wish. It is a lonely empty place. I choose not to for I still must retain the hunger of my flesh; to rub my shoulder and soak my foot and yet my hand is still free to scratch my cheek. I am thus busy, occupied with mutinous sounds of my budding distortions. To lust from that view to a perfect pair of cheeks has long since passed my calling-to this my flesh no longer responds, but for love it never ceases to rise, especially with the help from those love gases drawing me up from the fresh spring earth.

Who should come to love first? Can we plan to love together? My thoughts too often gather to accept that it is not possible. My annual spring Klooog is in constant preparation to connect. It has not taken root. Given the opportunity, it would; but then it would soon grow to choke the happiness that has not yet budded to flower. There must be a girl for me, but am I ready for her, as much, or more at times, if she would just show herself and wait? I've done all this before: my dog, my horse, my fishing pole, my boat. This clear bright morning sun, the soft movements of snowy clouds, caressing my sight, they will be love enough for me...and yet, sometimes a cold beer to help chase a nagging thought, joined with some good food and the cool smell of the fresh morning air. The birds playing for love. The jumping fish braving the deadly air to view the sun, then quickly falling back to life. The bittersweet memories from my youth replayed again for me, only better this time. I can talk now to God-that is love enough for me! I don't want any more. Let others reap and weep to find. I have enough. I don't need any more Klooogs-Its time to live! Sometimes I think I can still hear my mother calling me from across the lake when I was a boy, and I then have to smile. She left me all her love. I still have so much left to give. I know it's not a Klooog. It doesn't hurt a bit. Hold it! I think I got a bite!

Benjamin's favorite Klooog Story!

"TURNING BACK TO INSANITY"

To be empty again.
To prepare to receive what could become my fulfilling need is something I will accept to do again.
Soon I shall choose to begin to fast, perhaps until my end;
And on the sixtieth day, my mind shall float away from my flesh until the spirit is completely free.
I will then accept the reality before me and relive all the good that has gone past me.
Who could enter my thoughts that would hold me to this resolve?
The clock ticks on, advising me.
I cannot remain as I am.
My hand proceeds to move with this pen across paper.
I watch with satisfying curiosity the words that I could easily claim are mine.
Yet I am not sure,
I must draw back to reach for someone to journey forward with me,
I cannot again proceed alone.
How many times must I repeat, only to lose that person again?
Must I return the persons to their reality, to know to accept?
As I turn to speak again, he is no longer with me.
Each time I lose, someone else seems to prepare for me.
I try again.
Strangely, but now I seem to have two persons that appear to go forward with me, letting me realize I need them both.
Soon there may be more. My skill for this endeavor is increasing.
My mind seems stronger, my confidence grows.

Even I like what I've been writing now, perhaps well enough to claim it as my own.
I'm beginning to see that it is I who is perhaps moving my hand to paper. It may be from my mind and no one else's, but in the absolutes of reality I know it cannot be.
Shall I awake to find that the world is sane and I am not, or to a different nightmare accepting that
I'm alone in my understanding, looking for a partner, only to find the vast emptiness that surrounds me?
My greatest Klooog would be to go back.
I know I will.....

REALITY KLOOOG
(A CUP OF COFFEE)

Truth and facts have nothing whatsoever to do with reality. The answer of course, is true. The following parables emphasizes this. To this one, I could easily add numerous others from personal experiences.
A hungry traveler drives into a strange town, parks in front of an inviting looking coffee shop, enticed by a sign in bold bright letters saying:

FRESH HOT COFFEE 25 ¢ CUP

Entering, he proceeds to sit down on an old fashioned hard counter stool and orders a cup of coffee. When served, it is neither hot nor fresh, and when presented with the counter slip, he finds that it cost not twenty-five cents, but forty-five. He asks the counter-boy for an explanation for the disparity in price.
Discounting the truth and facts, the reality was what he had to deal with.

REALITY KLOOOG II
(IGNORING REALITY SOMETIMES KILLS)

A man crosses the street not paying attention to the sound or viewing the reality of an oncoming speeding vehicle. The truth is that he should have and could have stopped and looked as he has done many times before. He did not. The reality killed him...not the truth and facts. It was his distortion of thought that damaged his ability to perceive the reality that could have saved him...His death mainly attests to the truth and facts. The results became the reality...

GOOD WAITRESSES SOMETIMES GET KLOOOGS (SUZY'S STORY)

It was about a quarter to twelve Wednesday, June 3rd, at the old POUR M-N diner where I work. When in walks Mr. Rappaport for his usual Wednesday lunch date. His friend and former partner, Mr. Morris, hasn't arrived as yet. I remember that it was really clear and gorgeous, almost like a summer day.

"Mr. Rappaport," I asked. "Same table for two?"

"Yes, Suzy, thank you."

He seated himself in his usual seat at his favorite table against the northeast window. On Wednesday, I always reserved that table for him and Mr. Morris.

"Would you like to order now, Mr. Rappaport, or would you like to wait for Mr. Morris?"

"I'll just wait Suzy, if you don't mind."

I set the table with the usual fresh bread and rolls and filled the glasses with ice water. Mr. Rappaport seemed not to be aware of my fussing. His eyes were staring through the window. He was usually so talkative and friendly-like ya know! He appeared to be watching for his friend, Mr. Morris. Each time someone came into the diner, Mr. Rappaport would turn checking to see and returning again to look out the window. It was very unlike Mr. Morris to be late. I remembered him as nearly always arriving first, waiting for Mr. Rappaport. Richard Morris and Morty Rappaport have been meeting for lunch every Wednesday rain or shine for nearly seven years. Mr. Morris was 79 and Mr. Rappaport is past 80. Both lost their wives about three years after they retired. They both looked forward to their two-hour Wednesday lunch.

"Suzy."

"Yes, Jack" (He's my boss and counterman), "Old habits are

hard to break. Just see how he keeps looking at the old pocket watch."

"Suzy," Jack said sadly, "I know he's not coming." The two hours are nearly up.

"Jack, what was that big parade of cars about that passed through town this morning?"

Jack seemed about to answer when instead he turned and walked away without a word. The two hours seemed to pass painfully for Mr. Rappaport. He checked his watch again; knowing it was time for him to leave. He did not touch any of the bread and water on the table. He slipped five Dollars under the saucer. I never even left him a check. Their usual lunch tip was a dollar each. He was about to leave when I stopped to ask him if he knew anything about the motorcade that passed through town this morning.

"Yes, I do Suzy. It was a funeral for a good man. We both attended, only he's still there."

I haven't seen Mr. Rappaport since that day. But every Wednesday about lunchtime, I seem to find myself wishing he would come in and pick up this Klooog he left me. The poor dear old man. I wonder how he is. I sure miss him...

"DEAL ME OUT"-"I'M BUSY!"

It's April, I'm 54, and the year is 1984, the Place is South Fallsburg, New York. I'm on a roll and I know it! I must really be good. I seem to be able to write now from any emotional position. Out comes a movement to capture the readers mind that he may soon perceive the story as if it were his own. I know that I have been overly applauding myself, probably a danger in regard to the work. The response to the Klooogs has been overwhelmingly positive. The limited marketing job I can do here in South Fallsburg is encouraging. I expect to be finished with these Klooogs when I reach a magic number. When I hit it, I'll know. The Reality Questionnaire is nearly finished. I will need another three weeks on the parables and two weeks on the structure and further editing and then the book. The person who has helped me the most to get started again is a living, breathing, thinking, feeling girl. She is as real as the Klooog stories. Everyone will know her name if she will let me use it. Of course, there is her daughter to consider, perhaps it would be wise not to. The price of fame may perhaps be too high. When I was younger, it seemed that I needed to play every hand that was dealt me. I always seemed to win more pots than anyone else, yet at the end of every game of life that I played, I found myself a loser. I became an expert at dumping on myself. Things are better for me now! If I cannot raise myself together with my partner, I find it's a hand I can't play. Deal me out. I'm not interested in playing any more. Let someone else play. If winning means losing, deal me out. The game is full of Klooogs.

OLD KLOOOGS NEVER DIE

More than fifty years have passed, and yet these uninvited thoughts still come back to my mind. How I severely punished my little son for something that does not matter now.
God has since taken him from me.
More than thirty years have gone by, and yet I can sometimes hear his little voice bravely crying,
"But daddy, I didn't do it!"
I would not listen.
It is then that my chest pains, and my heart seems to stop...
My Klooog has come back!
It will come again...

KLOOOGS ARE NOT FOR EVERYONE

My name is Janie and I'd like to tell you how I got my Klooog. This happened just this afternoon. It's such a heavy that I felt, that I had to tell someone quickly to relieve the pressure, so I called my best friend Doris.

"Doris. Please, I know it's late and it's after seven...Thanks Doris. I'll do the same for you sometime...Oh, really Doris. I'm really sorry, but listen, he'll get in the mood again, he always does. He's in the other room now watching television; good. Doris this happened this afternoon. I had the kids home this afternoon because of the rain you know, and they're playing some silly game together when the phone rings-guess who, yup-Chet. Yeah, the guy who thinks he's in love with me-...No, Harry doesn't know about him. WHY should I tell him? He wouldn't care anyway! Anyway, the phone rings and it's HIM, Chet, Well I couldn't talk to him in the living room with the kids playing and carrying on-so I tell Joey the oldest to watch his little brother and make sure to keep him away from my antique shelf. I slip into the den and close the door and the conversation gets wild...Doris stop giggling...No I` am not going to meet him...besides, how can I? Besides, that is not what I called you up about to relieve my pressure. Well, I'm on the phone with Chet maybe five minutes or so when I heard a crash coming from the living room and the little one starts screaming. Naturally I had to cut my conversation short and put him on hold and in I run. Well! There's Joey standing holding both broken pieces of my expensive Meissen vase and the little one crying on the other side of the room. Well, you could imagine! After warning Joey! He tried to tell me he didn't do it. Now he's looking like he's lying. Well, Doris, I wailed the tar out of him. Boy was I mad! I rushed back into the den to finish saying good-bye to

Chet, when a few minutes later in walks the little one tears streaming, he comes up to me and tells me he did it, not poor Joey. Well, you can imagine how I felt after that Doris, I tell you. Kids are nothing but heartache. **Now**, I got a Klooog I feel I don't deserve and for what? It wasn't my fault-anyone can make that mistake; and now the little brat won't talk to me. I told him I was sorry and I would make up for it...No, he wants me to keep my Klooog-the little bastard. If he doesn't stop making me feel guilty, I'm going to wail the tar out of him again...You're right Doris, he'll get over it...Listen Doris, don't let me keep you, and thanks for letting me bend your ear so late. I'll do the same for you sometime. Talk to ya tomorrow."

HIRAM AND FIRE - `EM JONES

Hiram Jones worked for my father and then for me for over thirty-two years. He was the Godfather at my christening and was there at all my graduations; he also attended the christening of my son. How often I wanted to fire him after my father passed away! How strongly afterward he chastised me for not adhering to my fathers staunch devotion to integrity and honesty, and how often and unfairly I had admonished him! I secretly wished him to leave, but he tenaciously continued to ignore my inner projections. He did finally leave; God took him to a higher office as he was still working for me that afternoon. I now remember the patience, love and understanding he had provided to me in my childhood. Why do I now hear him chastising me, telling me he cares, caustically warning me to ponder the right? The payments due come now and then from these thoughts; but then they stop to accept the Klooog that has replaced him...

JUDGMENTS KLOOOG (WHAT'S IN A FACE?)

"Information viewed for Judgment renders the information useless"- On a beautiful, bright, warm, sunny, spring day.

A young lovely couple are enjoying a pleasant drive to visit an aunt who had moved to the country. Her instructions as to finding her new residence did not appear particularly clear nor explicit. The young lovely couple, bright and gay and happy decided to enter into the next driveway to ascertain as to whether they were in fact traveling toward what appears to be the right direction. The lovely girl gracefully slid out of the car, merrily skipped to the large white country house, rang the doorbell and a pleasant country smiling person came to the door. Explaining her uncertainty as to how she should proceed to arrive at her aunt's house, the man appeared happy at first to direct her. "When you get to the end of my driveway, make a right turn; then go straight down the road about two miles, you'll then come to a fork in the road. Bear left, then a quarter mile from the fork, you'll come to an intersection; at that intersection take a right turn, and you will be on her road".

The man appeared oddly strange to the lovely young girl. relaying the instructions to her companion, they proceeded down the driveway, turned right, came to the fork in the road, procrastinated and proceeded to judge the information given to them. The information became *useless*.

HAVE A NICE DAY!

A wise man sat on his rock of wisdom wisely viewing the politics of life. As his life progressed, his view became even sharper and his wisdom seemed even clearer. His thoughts prevailed upon him to accept that his life was indeed empty of purpose: given the opportunity to change the world, he left his rock of wisdom. In the confusion of being a fool, he soon sought to return to his rock of wisdom. He carried back with him the spoils and comforts from the politics of life. Each road that he took that could lead him back to his rock of wisdom seemed to detour him into yet another road pointing to opportunity. Gradually he shed his virtues. The years seemed to pass too quickly, finally in fear and desperation, he crawled back to his rock of wisdom, only the firmness of reality he had failed to perceive. He now understood that his wisdom came not from the rock, but rather from not allowing himself to being delivered as a fool. The payment is due. He can see it coming. Here you are Sir, your Klooog. Have a nice day!

A CHILD'S REALITY

A child viewed his television by day and by night,
In time the child was judged to be bad.
As punishment he was not permitted to view television for 2 years.
After 2 years, he was made to watch.
He got a Klooog,
He turned bad,
He was again punished,
He lost his Klooog!

THE SMOKERS KLOOOG-LOCKED UP!!

Smoke is the aftermath substance;
Its viscosity is minus zero.
You can see it-taste it-smell it-but try to hold it!
It is completely void of human substance,
But yet take another puff and try still again.
Without the soulful exercise of self-discipline, the human viscosity, like smoke, drops to minus zero.
What might have been life of great beauty and substance is now nothing but smoke.
Take another puff and think to watch truth filter through your nostrils.
The delusion is again complete.
The test for immortality begins too soon again.
The compulsion like that of the dog to biting his tail, becomes over-powering.
The delusion is a fantasy of a never ending spiral-
SMOKE!
I CAN'T STOP*!

*(The magic in a gift of words)

To discontinue smoking is most
certainly discomforting...
Not to abusive.
To continue: the abuse becomes endless.......

THE KLOOOG TO IMMORALITY

The government has taken it upon itself to form a bond of trust between itself on one hand, the patient, the medical profession, and the American Taxpayer on the other. All have suffered in this act of government positioning itself without proper checks and balances. In the end, all have had to make the immoral judgments. The end result is that we are all making payments from what could have been a productively viable system. The system is morally bankrupt. They invited immoral acts by disenchanting the medical profession with poorly structured Medicare and Medicaid checks and balances system. These distorted structures were soon fortified by its own indestructible regulatory agencies. The system soon invited the form-fillers to harvest as much wealth as human greed could comfortably and safely justify. Patient treatment applications are often presented for signature before actual treatment is begun, the patient never knowing what treatments are billed over his signature. Others in the medical profession were soon able to justify and rationalize at first small amounts of claims for unearned fees. As these irregular small amounts went unchallenged, the rest of the story has become the present reality. If a patient questioned this procedure or hesitated to sign a blank form (including insurance forms of all kinds), the patient would usually be told quite adamantly, "If you don't sign first, treatment cannot begin". Not always, of course; but the exceptions are so few as to truly comprise the exceptions.

Billions of dollars are being unfairly billed for payments, often for services either never performed, or worse, not needed. One may also proceed to look further down the line of government positioning itself to trust: defense contracts that allow for obscene cost over-runs, and then continue right down the line, to someone living quite close to you, perhaps to the other person in your mirror checking your smile...

TRUSTING KLOOOG

Two grown up women having been good friends, evolving back to their early youth, begin to each develop different life styles from their particular life's circumstances. They had remained good friends throughout their various life stages that time, emotions, and chemistry has a way of effecting. We shall call Woman # 1, Trusting, and Woman # 2, Dearfriend.

Several years had passed since Trusting lost her husband through a most difficult and long illness. A marriage of 20 years had not proved fruitful: A woman now in her mid-life, childless and at many times being quite alone. After her husbands death, she found herself thrust into the happy position of being busied, caring for a large well established, successful restaurant in Midtown New York. She found herself in that enviable position of being able to procure all the creature comforts one could develop a taste for. She became a free, happy, giving and sharing soul, never stingy for herself or those she particularly cared for. There came a time when circumstances did not go well for her friend Dearfriend. Her husband soon also passed away, leaving Dearfriend with two grown, but still dependent children. At her husbands passing, realities began to unfold that revealed financial burdens left in the aftermath of a ceased-to-function-poor-provider. Desperate and in need of immediate employment, Dearfriend informs Trusting of her difficult and present unhappy situation. After much harmonious complacent women chatter, it was decided that Dearfriend would take a full time position as cashier in Trustings elegant restaurant. It wasn't long afterwards that she became one of Trustings full time cashiers. Trustings allocated Dearfriend her choice of shifts. Several weeks had gone by and Dearfriend had adjusted to her duties in a proper and

cheerful manner. One evening Dearfriend was closing out her shift, preparing the tally for the next cashier.
She turned to Trusting proclaiming that she had forgotten to ring up for several sandwiches she had prepared to take home for her son. "Oh, don't be silly," Trusting explained to Dearfriend. "There is no need of that, take home some dessert you think your son may enjoy." Her position and its relationship seemed to proceed in a happy manner. One evening she found herself a little short funded for some incidentals she had intended to purchase on her way home. So she innocently borrowed $ 5.00 from her register drawer meaning to replace that amount on her return the following day. Unfortunately, the importance of the matter did not press her memory nor her conscience the next day or the day after and a new pattern of justifiable thought soon developed. Several months had gone by and Trusting was notified that her accountant would like to discuss what seemed to be a small figure disparity. The accountant had been working for the establishment since its opening. He was it seems properly named Suspicious, and Suspicious appeared to be definitely affected by the connotation of his name and he quizzically directed this fully to his friend and employer, Trusting. There in itself reflected into a mood for conflict. "Trusting," Suspicious gently implored, "There seems to be a small disparity in this months gross receipts relative to this months food purchase. Tell me Trusting, have you been checking the register receipts of all your cashiers?" Certainly, Trusting replied with great indignity. "And what about Dearfriend, that new cashier you put on several months ago? Have you been checking her register receipts as well." "Oh, Suspicious, why must you be so suspicious. I don't have to check Dearfriend," and so the matter was dropped. Several more months had gone by when now the disparity and the matter had again presented

itself to Suspicious. It has now projected itself as being quite serious. The short fall now was large enough that it could not be ignored. “Trusting,” he said, “Forgive me for acting so suspicious, for that is my name, but unless you check every register tape from this moment on, and you tell me you agree to do so, I cannot remain your friend and I will cease to do this work for you, and you will need to find yourself another accountant.” Faced with the reality that Suspicious was being quite serious, Trusting agreed to abide by his wish. The final results, of course, were quite devastating. Trusting did begin to check Dearfriends register tape and the revelations could not deny the source of great loss. This was, of course, not the loss of money, but the loss of a friend; Trusting had allowed herself to be placed in a position of having to trust, the results produced had lost her her friend. Her heart was broken, pieces from which would never heal; and, of course, the money was the least of that which was lost. Had she checked her friends register tape as she had done everyone else's, she would still have her friend and her money, minus the terrible burden of pain of this Klooog.

****

THE POWER KLOOOG

It's interesting to notice the intensity of people, determined to demonstrate the power they have to accomplish what they want, yet never really succeeding in achieving a personal fulfillment. They may prove through severe self-determination abilities of physical accomplishments. Still they seem to fail to provide for themselves what they so inescapably need. It is not determination that is needed in accomplishing this, but rather simply a new method of thinking that needs to be employed that would provide the view to personal reality. The greatest of mans achievements may well have been propagated through the broad scope of personal vision. The successful achievements were accomplished by the acceptance of a need, developed and completed only through the concept that logical computation equated itself to the reality at hand. The person who could swim or run great distances beyond what the ordinary person might consider possible, or perhaps lift great weights or climb great and nearly impossible heights, command a vast army or other force that he may have been responsible for, developing cannot be used to gather a personal want. He may also be the cogent adhesive that is holding this force of power. Yet all of these achievements that he has envisioned to accomplish and then succeed are never enough. Who knows him well enough to accept him as he really needs to be seen? The evidence is overwhelming, that this relationship, this joining with that perfect companion has eluded him. Perhaps it seems he has not been properly advised as to how he may invite such a person. The reality is that for him, no such person can survive within the scope of his fantasy. This is a special Klooog that follows and haunts him. Soon it shall be beside him; when he embraces it, it will be his end....

CAN A JELLY BEAN STOP A KLOOOG?

Everybody agrees with me-I must be right! Why else am I here? My wife looks at me at times, reminding me that my underwear rides up in peculiar places like everyone else's. She doesn't like where I am now. I know that she's sorry that I got into this entrapment of power. She's afraid for me and at times I imagine that she too will have to agree with me, for soon I will not listen to any of her deploration of excesses she seems to so easily view in me...things no one else dares upset me with. I wish at times I didn't love her so; I would then find it easy to be her president as well as everyone else's. I think I'm working at it. I know I will need a second term to accomplish this. I believe she knows this. She'll do everything to stop me, If she succeeds, I'll probably be better off. I'm getting too old now to be thinking I could be young enough to succeed. She has the power now to stop me. What is she waiting for? What if she changes her mind again and decides to let me run, and what if I run and win again?...PASS ME A JELLY BEAN, PLEASE; I think I'm getting a Klooog.

PAYMENTS OF THE CHILD
(Legacy to a Klooog)

There are words from my thoughts that I dare not write.
Words that would deliver me away from that important entrance to your mind.
If I could but enter your mind, locking myself into those passageways,
I would blow the blight that your distortions of thought have delivered you.
Natures way is to simply await the proper call to purify. As you agree to accept your last breath, there is always a child to try again.
To begin new, fresh, clean, free of human distortions. All are waiting on this beautiful new miracle to purify themselves by
nurturing and drawing, expounding always-always.
It seems to never change.
We need the child.
The child needs to accept our help.
It soon will make its payment.
It soon absorbs our knowledge, our thoughts; along with these thoughts,
come the fantasies-the misconceptions, the perversions drawn from fantasy-that must substitute reality.
These will be his payment for our help.

EVERYONE'S STUPIDITY KLOOOG

If a person were to appear to succeed in getting a right result by taking a wrong action, it would then appear illogical that he should take a right action to obtain a right result. Therefore, the impetus would appear that the wrong action must continually be employed. However, the wrong action which is continuing to travel, has no reason to stop and in time must return, negating the imagined right result.

The purpose of this book is to alter this worlds present direction, perhaps by just one degree.

Can you take a wrong action and get a right result?

You most probably think you can.
You do it all the time.
You just have to know how.
You're only human;
Certainly, everyone does.

The right answer, of course, comes from the waste of the cow's mate.*

*Correct Answer is in a Mirror Image

Bullshit

THE KLOOOG OF "WANTS"

You cannot empty your mind of what is not true without experiencing a sense of discomfort. Can you, the reader, go against nature's disposition of being drawn toward pleasure and away from pain? Does not a plant grow away from the cut? Will we not also? The reality is simply that it cannot be done. One cannot be expected to accept that view that he or she may in reality be in total malfunction.

This book reveals why a *total* transformation or realignment cannot happen; it reveals the impossibility and obvious fantasy of such an effort. However, the information given on the way is more than worth the trip, and the results will most certainly be positive.

The application of right information toward right action will enable you, the reader, to postpone the Conclusion that is before all of us. It is our divine right and privilege to choose that time in our minds and souls when we wish to return to the Original seed, and to do so with absolute human dignity and grace. It is this, then, so consecrated for all of us that we seek: The Postponement of Man's Final Conclusion. Let no man rob us of that right.

Most of us spend much of our productive and energetic years fighting and striving and crying in helpless futility, unable to mitigate, corral, subdue, or stifle our many undisciplined wants. The irrationality of it all! The immorality of it all! How many of us can look back to those occasional depressed moods, wondering what caused us to act so harmfully, so wastefully, so thoughtlessly, and particularly so helplessly? And how many of us have been able to change to the sturdier, safer position of logic whose safety lies so open to view and yet which so few can see? How many of us are willing to accept total responsibility for whatever circumstances we find ourselves in?

JUSTIFYING KLOOOG

My wife had accompanied me as we made several purchases in a building supply market. My wife had gotten quite familiar with my asking a particular question rather frequently and unexpectedly to total strangers, at least 8 or 10 times every day. We had concluded our purchase at Rickles, and were given our sales slip instructing us that the merchandise must be picked up in the rear of the store. Arriving at that point, a rather nice young man obliged us with quick and courteous service. As the service he employed for us was completed, I had casually asked him that question. "Michael, tell me is it possible to take a wrong action and get a right result?" The pleasant looking, respectful, polite young man turned to me and meditated several seconds and replied, "Nope, don't see how you can do it; no, don't know how it can be done." His answer gave me a lift; for it had been three days of asking that question now since I met anyone that said you cannot.

We then journeyed a short distance to a nearby competitor called Grossman and had gone through the same routine, made our purchases, got our slip and drove to the rear of the store. Again we had met another prime candidate for the question; this time the stock clerk was quite tall, with long flowing blonde wavy hair falling over his shoulders, and quite handsome and personable. He was courteous and cheerful and his attitude towards his work was quite refreshing. We spoke for a short time; he explained to me why he needed to wear his hair so long. He was often subjected to unfair personal judgment because of his appearance, but he casually informed me that he played in a rock band and that his hairstyle was necessary and expected. He helped load my station wagon with the lumber purchase and as he was about to depart I turned to him, (of course I knew his name from his nameplate on his shirt); I called him: “Scott, tell me, is it possible that you can take a wrong action and get a right result?” He turned to me; his eyes caught mine and held them for a moment. His reply was the one that was perfect and no one as yet offered me that answer: “How can you?” he casually replied.

The meeting and conversation with Scott gave me an emotional and refreshing lift and I thought to myself there must be more like him. My wife and I journeyed back towards home which is approximately 30 minutes away and upon arriving at our home, we noticed a good deal of activity in our swimming pool area. We were conducting our annual garage sale. Thinking some of our people helping with this event might need some assistance; I parked the wagon and proceeded to help with the sudden influx of interested buyers. One of the buyers I had noticed was a young Hasidic scholar. He had already made several purchases from one of my eager assistants, and they were now helping load his purchases into his station wagon. I approached and began to converse with him, soon learning that he was a scholar and teacher of the Talmud.

As he was about to depart, I again took that liberty to ask the question, “Tell me if you will, Rabbi can you take a wrong action and get a right result?” He looked at me and then up slightly as if he were communicating with an entity that belonged only to him; then he seemed to change his mind as if it were an improper question. Finally after long moments of personal meditation, he decided to look at me to reply. His answer was the most profound, in depth, lucid dimensional perceptive answer I had gotten thus far, and it was an answer I was not prepared for, nor was I aware that such an answer existed. Without this Rabbis answer I could not long have proceeded with this project. The wisdom of his answer gave the question a fresh dimension. I had been

CAN HUNGER STOP A KLOOOG?

My stomach is full. I'm not really hungry and yet I still seek a source of pleasure. Sex is not now available. Love has been held out of my picture for more than I care to remember. There is no one I care to have a conversation with. I no longer smoke; a drink has never proven itself to be anything more than an anesthetizer from one's reality. The pleasure has always proved itself to invite negative absolutions. Shall I look to experience the fruits from my imposed hunger again? Fasting? Would a proper and right purpose create that need? If there is, it would not matter, for I choose to ignore it.

If someone would just hold me again, perhaps lie with me to feel the others love life flowing separately and then together! Would that not be better than food or drink or smoke? Would that then be enough? It would be enough for me! Except-it has not properly been invited. I'm prepared to make the payment. Could I make the payment in advance? I think I would like to (if love were for sale). I would not hesitate to make the required payment. Unfortunately, the bill often comes in form of a Klooog-a Klooog that is not saleable. If it were, there are so many that I now have that I could make available, especially the one I'm expecting-HOLD IT! I think I hear her diesel driving up. Yup! It's her-how can such a beautiful girl turn into a Klooog? Easy! Love her and find out!

CAN THERE BE LOVE WITHOUT A KLOOOG?

What can I do? I need her and she is not quite sure how. The girl could not come to know how important she had become in my life. Every working fantasy predictable to reality is composed of and from my thoughts of her. Her speaking to me on the phone is enough to set me off. Every positive emotion of mine that is delivered up to me is accepting her presence in my life. She is my tug to love and then to life. Not knowing what is expected of me, I continue forward, blindly prepared to make the required payment for any wrong action. I listen for the sounds of negative conscience. I hear none. Have my ears suddenly gone deaf to the sounds of reality, or is the reality the sound of complacent harmony? I am in such desperate need of her, for she has become my hidden lead heroine in many of these Klooog stories; perhaps even more so, she has become the mediator to the reality I need to accept. She breathes, she cries, she laughs and giggles. She is constantly hungry or thirsty. When she eats, she looks like some cute squirrel. The stories are just a reflection. The reflection then becomes real and sturdy because of the radiant glow of this woman truly in love. Her radiance reflects her searching through the mirrors of life for someone to see her thus. Who should be the one to reach in and lead her out? If I then turn to face her, her reflection would be cast upon my soul. I would then be responsible for the love that would then be mine. These thoughts that are so real to me now must prepare me for the payments that will surely be due. A special Klooog is lying in wait somewhere. I shall look to avoid it. I can see her now in my mirror. Her tears are in my eyes. I know I cannot...she loves another.

MY WRITERS KLOOOG FOR NOT BEING A WOMEN

I have been given all the physical functioning male appliances that properly orchestrate that I am of the male gender. I often receive all the proper and necessary propensity to urges that rightly reflect this. I then must attest to that living reality of the male entity that is within me. I often try to rationalize the fantasy that I can speak through the feelings of a woman. I could not know from where her root feeds that nourishes her soul. To know, to feel, to be within her-to draw from her-to taste of her lips-to touch her body and hold it as if it should be mine-to drink full of her whispered words of love that feed my soul-to breathe for her-to listen and feel her life beat as if it were mine! For me, it is not enough! It is not enough! It is not enough for where I must now go with this pen. I cannot have the child that is mine. It is not yet mine; perhaps to become mine when my breath has accepted its final count and my flesh has left me. The child then accepts me without which I cannot know to provide words, a resolution to my words in the absolutes of honesty. Can some unique woman provide for me these feelings releasing the words I need? Is there such a woman? If there were, would she dare to exchange places with me? Would I then be capable of coming back, returning herself to her? Would I want to? If I could and did, and she could and would, would she give me back what was purely mine? None of this would then matter. I would then have what I need. I would surely be capable in dealing with the absolutes, which would be there for me. I could then lose this writers Klooog forever for not being a woman. I think I am getting a Klooog for even daring to write this.

I think instead I will need to listen to women more carefully, more deeply. It would help define thoughts I can accept to what is fantasy that so often passes for reality. I will try now to understand and to accept them totally and then to love them completely-always to deal with them nobly. Perhaps then they might accept me-deal with me nobly-love me completely and perhaps offer me what I need. It is all I can do. It is not enough! It never is-for there is my motive! That is the flaw! I demand absolute honesty knowing from this quest; I must answer to this subterfuge, to that personal motive. If it is a writer I must be, it is a Klooog I must suffer to accept...Except...I will not!

THIS LOVE NEEDS AN APPOINTMENT

Progressing forward sometimes means sitting still when there seem so many available means to travel elsewhere and partake of pleasure, all sorts of pleasure, all requiring payments; all will return us to where I now sit. Saturday I have a tentative appointment to make love-sex has not been written into the scene as yet. The players will be experienced with nearly all the negatives of life. That will be their burden. They will need much courage and delicate care to employ the proper tenderness and compassion to bring the virgin soul to surface. If this can be realized together, this appointment for love will singe the heavens. Ecstasy surely cannot be perceived as ordinary pleasure! This lovely tall dark slender feminine creature is certainly not ordinary. She is so far above the average man that she often lowers herself to her lowest level so that her words can be delivered from a truly even level.

This apparition is only physical. Can I hold her free of her negative emotions? Can I strengthen her enough so that she becomes able to hold me in release of my own that would have us lose the purpose that has drawn us towards this appointment for love? I will need to feel the pain of wanting to be with her again to make the proper payment, knowing that our meetings will be fewer and perhaps become less fulfilling. The pain from this thought may become more than I can bear, but from this great pain of having to accept the loss of her, I will find myself able to write. I believe she has the power as a woman to truly make love to me. Will I have the necessary compassion to humbly accept it? From this writing until our future meeting, I will not know. She must be my guide. I believe in her....

THE TRAP OF DECEPTION

I'm in desperate need to know!
It seems that I now have a personal dilemma to deal with.
She pulled a fast one on me Thursday:
She appeared so damn inviting,
I must say I found her to be very womanly. (meaning beautiful).
Before I needed her, which was okay:
Now it seems that I want her.
There are questions she would answer for me.
If I want her
I must get rid of this want or simply disconnect before it is too late.
I need to ask her to advise me;
She will know what to do.
Why must she be so damn honest with me?

SMALL DOWN PAYMENT - 60 MONTHS TO PAY!

I would like to get a Klooog lusting for a very special woman who could be available to me. I would certainly then have something from someone, which could pain to work off other illusionistic frustrations. I might not be in the position I am now, safe, relaxed, out of the pouring April rain. When I'm there, I yearn to be here. How odd, I now do not have that burning desire to possess one of the most sensuous and elegantly charming, intelligent women I could ever hope for. Yet, I smile awaiting to know her positioned response to my profound and puzzling request which I'm sure she has muddled through and rejected more times than my safe and sound ego cares to view. Still, I would be curious to study my own response as she is considering and weighing her positive emotions against the probable negatives that might come up. She certainly has a pleasant looking body, but if it could not give off any love to me, it would not serve our need. I must consider her feelings very carefully for she is a vulnerable as I. Perhaps we are looking for a common denominator-one that we can both draw to, a power source for the positive emotions we so often find ourselves in short supply of. I believe she would agree to lend herself to me in any way which her conscience would allow-something I care not to manipulate. I needed to have the anticipation of believing she could be mine, if even for the shortest period from her life. Marilyn, a name that was well chosen for her. Her name gives off meaning to me. She is a mysterious leader who runs divinely to love, too often finding herself perplexed in conspiring to utilize two directions at the same time. In the end she makes her payments and she learns. She has earned her knowledge with more tears than this page can hold. I need this from her, this knowledge of love. I do not know why she should give this to me, or what her reasons would be for either direction, but whatever they are, I will accept knowing that I can continue for a time and write further. I have wisely chosen to elevate her to such heights that lying on the ground, she would be tall enough for any man. I'm waiting for her now, what she will be wearing will give some clue. I need and love the anticipation of love. I certainly won't need a shovel for this one. I'm happily digging this hole without one. When I fall in, whoops! I'll have my Klooog...60 months to pay!

MY KLOOOG SAYS NO! MY HEART SAYS YES!

Please don't start making plans. The person doesn't fit the slot. She comes on great, but what does she want. She's a living, breathing, feeling chemical factory. What chemistry is she mixing for me tomorrow? Can I accept or deal with what's coming up? Who needs it? I want this; she wants that. How can I equate? We both seem to be looking beyond each other. What does she see beyond me? What do I see beyond her? I want her love, loyalty, her mature approach to life, and sometimes her silly giggle to shake me loose from this pervasive mendacity of mine. I want her eyes looking into me again, telling me she accepts me, that her mind accepts me, her love accepts me, that she knows all about me; and that it doesn't much matter. When she is agreeable to all these things, would she also in time agree to tenderly accept me inside of her? Will not my want of her at times seem to end? Will she not demand also the same of me? What if I am not there for her in those due times of her rightful demands? Will I again curse this unremitting stupidity as the cause for my losing her again? Can I hold her for understanding these differences within us? Could it be that this would be the flaw that could end us? Must we go through this pain and helpless anguish again and again? Is it worth it? My coming Klooog tells me no! My logic must agree! No matter...I'm lost...I love Her!

I asked her softly if she would. She did not answer. Instead she began to slowly remove her clothes. I could smell the odor of her. It was pleasant. She was clean smelling and pleasing to look upon. I watched her with curious fascination as she stoically delivered me of my request. As my request of her was completed, she turned to face me. Staring stone faced; she then proceeded to walk in the direction of my bedroom. She was indeed a geometrically delicate and feminine creature. This lovely view of her walking away had now completely replaced this pervasive gloom of mine. I removed my clothes and soon followed her. She had covered herself with the thin cover and remained rigidly still, her eyes opened, staring stone like at the ceiling. I lifted the cover; she accommodated my space on that small single bed, and I, too, found myself staring soundlessly at the ceiling. Our bodies could not help but touch. There were no words, just the angry beat of her heart. It was a long time before she spoke. I had become aroused, but made no move to accommodate this urge to be within her.

"Mr. Benjamin, you can if you want to. I really don't mind."

"I couldn't," I heard myself hoarsely whispering.

"Is anything wrong? Why did you ask me to remove my clothes? I know you want to."

"My wish was to be with you as we are now doing." I again gently whispered. Her smooth, young body now began pressing gently closer to mine as we both stared up at the ceiling. It was both pleasant and peaceful. "I needed to feel that there could be love between us."

"What about my needs Mr. Benjamin, your body feels pleasant to me and your flesh is arousing me. I didn't think it would. Mr. Benjamin, I really like the feelings I have now

for you, I feel so silly!"
"Please tell me why are you giggling.:
"I just cant help it. Mr. Benjamin, you never even asked me my name."
"Its not important. Besides I already know your name. Its ________________."
"Yes, but how did you know, Mr. Benjamin? I'm not really sure, but I think I love you. I feel something nice for you. Would you mind very much if I were to lie on top of you? I would like to look at your eyes." I did not answer. My heart was beating wildly as she gracefully moved her long slender body over mine. I could not now contain myself. My need would by definition soon transfer itself to an irresistible urge to be safely, desperately within her. I did not expect her to be so delicately graceful in her movement to me. My passion was begging to reach a peak as she looked down to me and into my eyes. I felt myself entering paradise when a single tear fell from her eye into mine. It was over. My eyes blinked open. The nightmare was suddenly upon me. She was gone! I again reached for her only to now grasp the emptiness of the terrible Klooog she left me. I wish she would come back to me sometimes when I'm awake!

TRUDY AND HARRY KLOOOG

Two people meet and appear to have fallen in love. Perhaps in reality they may have fallen in love with an image of their imagined self-perfection. A subjective perspective may not permit a proper view. Many people tend to fall in love with themselves. How often have many of us found ourselves entrapped into bizarre, difficult and most unhappy situation, fantasy becoming replaced in the guise of reality.

How often have you been able to accept the reality that had been invited to provide the needed solution? This is a rather short story about two *imaginary people.*

Please accept also that this story is a fantasy. I state this because it may appear to be so identifiable to so many. Once upon a time, two people named Harry and Trudy fell in love. It was a short but magnificent courtship. Every courtesy, every tenderness was extended to one another. Nothing appeared too difficult or unremitting to sacrifice for one another's contentment. Each placated and respected and coveted the others fantasy. The fantasy, of course, being what one had expected of the other.

Harry was a man one might accept as being fragile, tender introvert, whereas the one thing that confused him more so than his ability to understand reality was his inability to perceive and understand a relationship of love. Being a person that one must view as constantly prepared to compromise a stressful situation, he willingly forgives and overlooks the obvious and oncoming conflicts that appeared to develop.

Trudy was not that far removed from Harry. What she couldn't see or understand or identify in so much as Harry was concerned, was her inability to fulfill from her thoughts those aspirations that seemed connected to *her* fantasies of love. This state of affairs certainly seemed to be directed down towards that narrow crowded path of much unfulfilled expectation. It was not long before certain key fantasies painlessly faded especially during some of those pervasively disappointing sexual encounters, which in time became happily less frequent. All seemed to give way to the obvious profusion of abundant and genuine love.

I thought I'd include a bit of caustic truth so that perhaps some of this reality could be accepted with a much needed sense of humor. Ah, to be able to erase all of life's past negative actions invited by the continuing applauding of ones personal mendacities. Must we all go forward to commit the same negative pervasive mistakes over and over and over again? It appears that we will.

Trudy on the other hand was far more realistic. She secretly accepted and knew all his faults, but at first was completely unaware of or unwilling to accept and recognize all of her own. Would you all like to know what Trudy secretly thought and felt and perceived insofar as to project what she no longer expected of poor Harry? For one thing, it was obvious she could never do successful standing ovation while urinating and so she more often sat down and did the best she could. She never accurately judged her inability to perform as a male. Her most debilitating judgment to this on the other hand was reserved for poor Harry. Can any of you in all honesty sit down and tell me what this all means? Perhaps if you were to realize the purpose of this conversation, you may certainly be in a better position that I for observing from your own perspective the determination as to why and how Trudy and Harry clung to each other right up to and beyond their fiftieth wedding anniversary. They were often asked what was their secret? The secret may have been that they tenaciously tended not only to judge each other, but rather to equally and secretly judge themselves. What this book needs is a smile and if you're not smiling, throw the book away. There's no hope. Surely there must be a little bit of Trudy and Harry in every marriage. Can you recognize the mendacity in this story from some of the times in your life?

A VIRGINS REPRIEVE
"WHAT'S THE USE!"

Would you if you could?
If you would, could I?
If I could, would I?
If I could and I would, would you still want to?
What if you would and then I didn't?
By the time we did I probably couldn't.
But if I did and I could,
Could the pill be a placebo?
Couldn't it?
But what if we did and it...
"Henry**, Please would you just shut up and take me home,
I'm getting a Klooog!"
"You are?" "______________!"

**Not all Henry's are alike!

I watched her without emotion as she began to slowly dress herself.

"We aren't going to see each other after this."
I heard my voice reach into her, realizing too late how it cut. She looked at me with that sometimes-special look she often reserved for when she felt that she may have lost something important in her life. Something or someone was being taken away; this loss of an important possession. She had not planned it happening. I did not leave her the choice this time. It was I who was calling an end to this suffocating relationship. This important decision was not made in the court of her control. I knew this. It was my move. My serve. I volunteered to accept the payment that she reflected back to me. Perhaps it was just as well. She turned, looking directly into me; her reply came back to me in her most caustic tone:
"You're right."
It was her turn! It cut the same. What are we doing? Were we speaking and acting just for effect? For what purpose? To deliver some obviously achievable negative. The pain was beginning to swell in my chest. It was growing to unbelievable intensity. She was completely dressed now. There was no stopping these movements to conclude this relationship. I never quite prepared myself for the pain that followed my planned disconnect. The flesh from the spirit crying to re-connect-to be lost again within her female spirit. I could not agree to be locked within the walls of her soul for all eternity. My mind-That damn logic-My choice of what I then had to choose as right became too much. I had tried countless times before to break away-each time I found I needed her anesthetizing presence to break the

unbearable pain of not being with her. I had almost given up trying. The pleasure of her, seemed to be worth any price demanded-except that the payments had been killing me. I no longer seemed to have an identity that surely had to be mine. I must fight for that. If I don't I would have nothing. I knew that in time she would not return to what was then left of me. I could no longer identify with the person she once had espoused to love. The reverse also appeared to be so. All the compassion that was in me, the compassion my mother endowed me with, was now in bitter conflict. The terrible unfeeling and uncaring actions of deeds we performed to test our independence were delivering us to this finale. We had lived together all these unbelievable months, made searing and passionate love, countless and memorable times, with no commitment other than satisfying our immediate needs of each other. She picked up her several small bags and left without a word. I called back to her through the open door and asked her if she would like to have a last good-by kiss. She shook her head without turning and continued out of my sight. The emptiness that overwhelmed me then captured my life's flow, rapidly draining my chest. I ran after her in a maniacal panic. She had forgotten one of her bags. I shouted after her. She stopped and turned. There were tears in her eyes. She shot me down again.

"If you don't mind, would you just answer one question for me?'

"George, what do you want from me now?"

"I would like to know if you are really dumb enough to say yes if I asked you to marry me."

"George, the answer is no!"

"Why?"

"Are you really asking me to marry you?"

"Yes, dam-mit, I am asking."

"Well, for your information, I am not dumb enough for that, but I am smart enough to say yes!"
"Why would you want to say yes? I never told you I love you!"

"Then why would you ask me to marry you?"

"Because I am not going to wake up tomorrow morning to say good-bye to you again. I want it stopped."

"Me too."

"What does `me too` mean?"

" Me too, means yes, you jerk!"

She was smiling, tears flowing down that loving silly face. Wc hugged and cried that morning; one month later we separated. Our separation seemed to be built in. We couldn't meet that next payment again. She married another soon afterwards. I'm very happily married now. I love my wife and adore my kids. I could never intentionally do anything that would hurt them; I know that I will always love HER. At some special times when I least expect it, I again see her funny beautiful smile, her tears flowing in my mind; how often they exit to flow from my eyes, knowing she will always feel the same way to me. This Klooog that has replaced her will always be there. It is my secret Klooog...it will never leave me....

SPEAK NOT OF KLOOOGS
LOVE'S INNER VOICE

We need to find a quiet time between us, time when all the important words for preparing harmony between us have joined. These will be our best times. It will be during these times that we can draw from one another emotional nourishment that will be open and full like so many nipples of a sow. There is so much emotional energy between us that needs to be properly distributed. It can only be realized from those quiet times. If we could learn between us how best to use less voice, allowing the soul to whisper through the voice, so that the voice itself can be enjoined to be caressed by the whispers of love drawn from the soul! The voices inner inflections from other times of our lives must not be used between us. The slightest negative note of sound inflecting to words can set us apart to wondering, losing again the quiet time we will need. Love requires oneness; no sound that could reflect another's negative testing need be heard. There is a quiet sound to be listened for that would constantly succeed in speaking if it were not for the voice of so many others that conflict to jam that which is ourselves. I sigh to know that you will understand. And yet these words will be important to you, this thought feeds my energy. It will be our common denominator. It will be words that we can both hold to during those times when the strong winds of conflict cover us up with the dust of despair. No gimmicks other than our gaze to each other will be needed. Strip yourself of all that hides you from us-only then can we be truly covered with what is ourselves. Know me for what I am; touch me for what I am, and you will see that I am truly no one else. Let me so thoroughly strip myself to view that there can be no shadow of doubt that there is no one else to view but I before you. Touch me and know there is no one else that you are touching that is intermixed with me. We will then know what it is to be one, and for brief moments we can exchange places to view and feel from the other what we are as we return. Love's inner voices will require endless conversation. These will be the quiet times between us. When they are gone from us, and we are gone from us, no other pain could matter; and I shall molt and cry and look again for a perfection that was between us. All will know me then by the Klooog that has replaced you. All through the crowds of my life, I shall once again look for your face, but I will only find a face and you will not be there. When we cannot seem to find us any more, I will still have myself and this new feel of my life. I am full of love and it is spring again...

"I love my Peugeot, but hey, ya wanna know what my next car is gonna be? Guess!"

"I give up."

My answer was somewhat caustic in its tone, being able to now accept a clearer view to the reality of this soon to be faded relationship. My real-life emotional character model for those many Klooog stories and purgation's of thought would need to end at the moment of her departure. Her answer returned to the question she volunteered to me was:

"A Jaguar."

And of course, when she moves to another place, she then will get a dog. When I had added up all her words, I then knew that she was indeed a fantasy in my writer's imagination. My logic was that it was time to disconnect. She had become my emotional appliance. An important appliance that was needed for me to begin writing again. Her fading dream of happiness was the Monte Carlo. This tattered dream soon transferred itself to another fading fantasy, again creating a fantasy projection towards happiness. The Peugeot diesel was not thoroughly prepared to replace her fading happiness (it was already beginning to fade).

Her next fantasy appliance to happiness would seem nearly impossible to acquire. This would, of course, be the Jaguar. The release from this writer's fantasy had now been accomplished. This was realized from my being able perceive this correct information. This viewing to me of her thoughts-to happiness, exploded the fantasy within me. Revelations from this lovely, delicate creature as to her never ending wants returned me to reality. I had kissed her countless times in my mind, delivered from my emotional encompass as a man. I embraced ecstatic thoughts of love, but ever in my mind, never accepting to enter within her chambers for love. She was my appliance, as her Peugeot is to her. When she revealed to me that her new fading fantasy to happiness would need to be replaced by a Jaguar, fortified by moving to new quarters and then further to be fortified by the acquiring of a dog, it made me realize that I needed to replace her with the reality that was mine to accept. I accepted!

Had I from my writer's inspired imagination transferred the fantasies of her to personal living reality, I would have needed to have entered into the nightmare of her shifting sands of thought that delivered to her those projected distorted views of happiness. How easy and refreshing and safe and strengthening this viewing and accepting of reality had suddenly become for me. My soul was returning to its rightful owner. Needless to say in the more than 10 months of sometimes typing but mostly using her as a personal sounding board, this in-depth platonic relationship with this lovely tall dark charming slender girl developed into a most important needed human appliance providing me with emotional stimulation for the emotional brain energy that I needed to write with. I have never physically embraced her (although I imagined it many times). If I had, she would not be down on paper, but rather would be in and out of my bed. (I believe in time I would have felt cheated). None of the words I needed to write could have been progressed to paper without her. That Saturday night I gave her a few small tokens of my appreciation, walked her to her Peugeot, waited for her light to go out on her diesel dashboard, said, "So long," closed the door, and then I knew, *So long is notta Klooog!*

HELLO KLOOOG! GOOD BYE LOVE

I shall now begin a story that no one seems to have an ending for. It would seem appropriate that the ending will be when I choose to draw my last breath.

The year was 1955. Perhaps one might accept that it was the autumn of my life for it was also the autumn of that year that I chose to say good bye to a girl.

No one person at that time of my life had yet deprived me of so much that had been purely mine. I said good bye to a girl that had been purely mine. I said good bye to a girl that my spirit and chemistry insisted that I must possess, yet my mind and my seed said "No!" My chest cavity cried for help- But I could not stop the pain. I drove her home to Brooklyn that night, knowing I could not and would not see her again. The execution of this revelation delivered a degree of pain and anguish that I could not then properly describe. How could I? How could I have been objective, thinking through the quagmire from those distorted perspectives? It was a crippling subjective time frame for me. It lasted many years afterwards. For the sake of providing this valuable Klooog story, I must force my memory open to deliver her name: "Lilia Bornofsky." The Lilia Bornofsky of Brooklyn could not deal with the quality of truth that had been so important to me. I could equally as well not deal with the fantasies of her reality. What a predicament to find ones total young pervasive wants tied to. I was flying like a bird whose sturdy feathers had suddenly lost their position of purpose. I was 10,000 feet in the air with powerful winds and suddenly having no feathers. My heart was beating my chest to a deafen ing shattering inner silence of pain-pain that traveled up to that vast space between my ears. It was then I became severely blinded by tears delivered from painful terror. My chest fighting my heart to stop-to end this pain-only my fear of greater pain provided the urgency to continue. Relief did not come. My past army leadership training had installed this insidious propensity to resist all mendacity...it was this resistance that focused me to this unbearable want, that urgent desperate want I could never deliver myself up to. I needed someone. Why could I not accept her? I could not fantasize to create a person in her that cannot live in my reality.

If I did, would it not end my want of her? Perhaps! Could I not then have awaited my needs to have given myself the time? It might have ended my desperate want of her. The pain would have stopped, replaced in time perhaps by something even less bearable. My sense of right was then too strong. I would not give in. My tenacity to hold to my reality would not permit that compromise. The resulting action had to be "Good Bye Lilia"-Hello Klooog!

I had then been in position of great inner strength. Still I chose to squander it to positions of great unknown weakness. The pain has long since vacated itself from these thoughts. But if I were but to have the proper wisdom of words capable of properly advising others, I would re-roll the camera of my life for a positive retake. The fork in my road would then have posted a sign up ahead, "Smile, you have just left Klooog-Love is just ahead."

Hello Love-Good Bye Klooog.

THE KLOOOG OR THE FANTASY?

I project that you may not be right for me. Yet you excite my emotions to life, that no longer seem to work for me. I know now that I need you. I seem not to be fully alive until those moments when I can be with you. It seems that now everyone else seems to have become unimportant. I have a need to see that beautiful silly, sometimes dopey face of yours. I eagerly await to hear again your lovely voice, sometimes words that tickle my mind; but most of all, I need to feel, to know your whispered closeness-from lips telling me that they are mine, silencing themselves for the love of me. Your gentle kiss can forever hold that secret message telling me all I care to hear. What else can there be for me? Your loveliness electrifying me once again to life? It is these connections from you that I need; without it, I know I cannot write. I must tell you these things so you know of your value to me. These thoughts are truer than my words can describe. You have become for me the beautiful mystery of life that unravels these words on paper. It is from this that I can now write. If these words could work their wonders, they would reveal a changed world where we would then be making love in all its corners. Every hour of every day that there is left for us would not be wasted with foolish words. We would be dissolved into the fulfillment of all that the ecstasy of love can hold. If I were to suddenly awake and reach for all this, would you again be denied of me? I know that it would be too much. Soon I shall sleep where you may once again come to me in my dreams. Could I survive the shock that happiness would reveal in finding you there when I awaken? It would be too much. I surely would be lost. Now I must accept this needed longing of a reality from which these feelings can draw. Should I dare exchange it for the Klooog that would be mine? Is this dream of fantasy better than the tasting of the reality of your sweet flesh, the sigh of your warm breath, the feel of your smooth breast caressing my chest, your lips touching, pounding my heart. I'm a fool, I know. The Klooog? Or Fantasy? Are you wiser than I? What would YOU choose?

LOVE'S KLOOOG
WHERE IS THE LOVE?

She's very much like you in every way, as everyone else is like you in every way, except she is not you! Holding you, feeling you from within tells me she cannot be you; for if she would be you, you would be a fantasy, and I would be again toying with the insanity that is in me. Where you come from, where you are now. The path leading to your rainbow of happiness delivers itself from another world. Your directional compass shows no similar harmony of purpose or resolve. All else to view must be a fantasy. Help me to let you view the reality of who you are, not who you believe you should be, or can be, or expect to be. Must we be eternally trapped into transforming ourselves from fantasy? It appears that our happiness lies in our ability to exchange one distorted fantasy for another. Who can deceive ourselves better than we? If we are unable to build a misconceived trap for us to fall into, there always seems to be some handy person close by who can be made to volunteer for this distorted service. It becomes so easy to transfer the Kloog responsible. In place of all that is right comes conflict, blame, some lust, bitterness, disgust, despair, and then the greater tragedy, the notion or urge for another poorly conceived quest for fulfillment and happiness. Another fantasy! The inviting of a new life to again become structured and built with sturdy muscles and bone and sinew rooted in the endless shifting sands of human fantasy. How easily we sift our lives through the sands. What holds those sands together? Must it not be all our tears? Soon, soon, there will be no more. God! *WHERE IS THE LOVE*? No more tears-No more tears!

"FEAR"

(The evil Klooog)

Evil requires a following
Fear attracts evil
Evil builds its power thru fear

Love's flower - withers thru fear
All intelligence comes thru love
Without love there is no intelligence

Freedom is everything
With fear there is no freedom
Intelligence cannot operate under fear
One cannot live with oneself with fear

Evil is the residue of fear
Love cannot flower thru fear

Without love
There is no life

God where is the love-
No more tears
No more strife
No more fears

Fear is the devils advocate
Love dispels fears

All evils come from the lie
See into the lie as a lie
Poof-Fear is gone

The devil finds another advocate
God is the poof we need to find
Speak up-not down

BEWARE THE DEVIL'S SMILE
THE DEVIL'S VOICE
THE DEVILS EYE

FEAR... OUR WORST KLOOOG Inspired by a good Irish lady named Ruth

THE FINAL KLOOOG
*LOVE IS...

Let me dream each nightmare sober,
That I may awake to know it is over,
Or accept to view that nightmare,
Accepting!
To close my eyes and it is over.

I was!

I Cared!

I Lived!

I Loved!

I tried!

I Cried!

I Had!

I Sleep!

I Gone!

Why? Why? Why? Why? Why? Why?

Because-Because-Because-Because-

***Illusion...**

THESE KLOOOGS ARE MINE

As I started writing this finishing page for the Klooog stories from my life that has been presented before you, I should stop wondering "Is there something I can do better that I failed to take notice of?" I haven't had much fun these past few years. The problem is that I've been able to achieve nearly everything that I set my thoughts and energy to and I've been overly successful in realizing that it all means nothing without someone to take that ride and know there is a kindred soul lying beside me. I cannot and do not see that in the offering. I believe there is nothing I now possess that I can perceive is of any great personal value. Therefore my liability of loss does indeed appear quite insignificant. If someone were to suddenly come into my picture again to provide a soul that could nourish my need to view what I've been missing, my fear must be instantly for its loss. All the Kloogs are in reality me. They will become my most precious and valuable possession of life. They belong to me and no one can claim that they are not mine. But they are yours too. My payment would be that you accept them and use them for right. The Klooog stories will be the cornfields I never planted, the horses I no longer have that were part of me, my dog, and my cat that are gone; my wife, my children, property, cars are truly insignificant. My Kloogs have replaced them. Looking and tasting of them proves to me the significance of the insignificance they now hold for me. The Kloogs will ring around the world. For me I know they will make the difference. At the time I did not completely understand why I wrote them, but I know now that they will help millions of people throughout the world. They will begin to help form a human bond of understanding through the humanity that is reflected from reality that is so deeply rooted in *all* men, and women! If there is more I can do, I shall await my next signal.

MY LAST KLOOOG
(ALL TO FAMILIAR)

My Life Is A Book That Ends To Soon

My life is but a blink in the universe. In this vast proposal of time as my blink concludes another will be awaiting, ready to take off at the end of my life's runway. My time for so long seemed endless; only now do I see how little time I am in total.

My son, how he hoards his time away from this nest of imperfections, implanted through the distortions from my youth. Each changing of the day draws his spirit further and further from me. Yet, I know he must return. What I do for him is so important-something perhaps no one can care to view. There is none capable to do what I fear I know-and yet never knowing if I can. Soon he will be upon me again, demanding a perfection in me I no longer hoard to possess. It lies now within him, and he is not sure. It becomes so well hidden in the folds of his youthful vigor, rushing to taste all that life has to view that needs tasting. He will love me yet, to a view from which I could only hear his voice from beyond; yet I know I will hear it. He has such power, harnessed with a disciplined direction of absolute, to rightful purpose. Yet it is his life that I must let him lead, watching the goodness, the greatness that lies so well protected from the never ending wants of his tender youth. Beneath lies his power. I would not know how to use it, but it is his now and not mine. He wastes it, as surely as I would abuse it. These focused realities give me peace. I have long since delivered myself from those delusions of happiness I once had. I refrain from doing so much, accepting that too often life's best profits are to be gathered by holding still; This festering can then begin to find some small quiet love close by. I will end this hour to write soon enough. But to whom am I writing you ask? It seems as if I'm writing to myself. Who else best understands what I have offered to say? But thank you for joining me. It will soon be my last line that I write. But please let me continue-a dear friend, Paul Messanger, gave me this line one day before being picked up by his Creator, "Life is often like a book, before you know it-you've come to the last page and it's over." There is so much we need to re-read, some with great happiness and tears, others with deep and shattering sadness. There must be a balance or we would lose the courage to go forward. But all is too familiar. The book cannot be changed, only re-read. All is too familiar. I need to make new pages to read, but my book is coming to an end. Have I not said enough too often? I think I have said too much. If I could buy back words I have spoken, if my wealth were a million, there would be at least that many I would pay to withdraw. But it is something that I accept can not be done. I've given birth to too much that has grown away from my control. I dare not look up, to mark the time to when my blink is due, but I will be told soon enough. Perhaps afterwards, they will then send me out to play, to go roller-skating again, or give me my first bicycle, or take me swimming again, or go out there and look for a good marble game again, or maybe release me from the Army to go home again, or find me my doctor friend who came rushing over to make house calls again, or stare with my penny into the vast assortment of candies awaiting my penny choice, or coming home to hug my first puppy. Keep me away from these tears in my life. I don't want to re-read these pages again. They're so worn that I can hardly make out my tears again. Yet these new ones are so easily available. I can never seem to skip those pages by lately. Soon I'll just close the book to let it rest on someone else's shelf of life! **All is too familiar...**

INSIGHTS FOR VACATING KLOOOGS

"BENJAMIN'S PURGATION'S OF THOUGHTS."...

EXORCISING THE MIND - RE-OPENING MANY UN-USED CIRCUITS OF THE BRAIN
SEARCHING INTO THE MEMORIES OF YOUR GENES
IS A MEANS TO AWAKENING INTELLIGENCE

YOURS...

The Klooogs often causing pain, in fact may not be yours directly - but may be locked in from a gene from some one else's past life's experience (memories in your genes)

GUILT IN THE UNIVERSAL HUMAN BRAIN

SURFACING THE KLOOOG TO VIEW ENDS THE CURSE...

A PURGATION OF THOUGHT

A phrase drawn from an Al Capps comic strip, Li`l Abner describes an important theme of this book. It is a cartoon scene where Mammy Yokum looks up to Li`l Abner and says, "ya know, son, it ain`t watcha know that gets ya inta trouble, it's all the things you know that jest ain`t so."

The purpose of this book is simply to provide through correct information, a means and method which could allow you, the reader, to empty your mind of those things that are simply not true. Fact, reality, and fantasy travel along the same emotional brain circuit, each a separate entity of thought, each needing that separate total sum of the entire emotional brain circuit. If your mind is not further occupied with the emotional energy needed to sustain countless misconceptions, then the means can be provided to persuade the reader that absolute honesty does in fact invite good luck and increase natural intelligence.

LUCK

HOW DO YOU INVITE IT?

No sooner do you father a lie to create a misconception than it at once owns you and it is you who must then assume responsibility for it. It becomes and is your creation. It will require your intelligent brain energy to sustain it, and maintain personal relevance to it, long after others have disregarded it. The hold it has never quite seems to let go. It becomes a damaging agent to natural intelligence. Therefore, the assumption is indeed correct: absolute honesty *does* increase natural intelligence and invite good luck.

LOVE

Love becomes blind to all negative emotions. It is the mother of all positive emotions. Without its continuous current, all other positive emotions would soon lose their beneficial function. Love has the uncanny ability, properly applied, to effectively neutralize all negative emotions. It has been demonstrated to be capable of being the most efficacious means of healing, particularly when all other means seem to have failed. The vacating of this emotion from plant or man or animal has been demonstrated to be quite capable of terminating a normal life span through some inner focus. This can be avoided by the proper use of Exorcise Formula. Love becomes reseeded through the emergence of reality, but indeed, becomes quite fragile in the world of fantasy. All positive human development nurtures and grows from this necessary emotion.

TEMPER

Temper is, of course, a most negative emotion. It is an emotion that at once shuts off that special valve in the mind that focuses reality to a dim view. It temporarily becomes capable of developing a barrier blocking all beneficial positive emotions. Actions vented from this emotion indeed become wrong actions, un-mistakenly inviting a wrong result. Results of these negative actions most often are delivered to the wrong person, at the wrong time, for the wrong reason, in the wrong way-and of course in the wrong place.
The results are always undesirable.

ANGER

I say: bottle it, cork it, store it. Let it have access through another emotion before venting to action and it may indeed prove at the proper time to be quite useful. Properly used, it may not be entirely a negative emotion. It may indeed become the catalyst to a vortex in time that may develop a right action. It is certainly a most untrustworthy emotion. This emotion could easily be given access to temper...

Bottle, cork and store your anger. It will serve you better un-vented -best that it be kept on a short leash. In the world of human realities, it becomes recognizable as the most subtle and entrapping catalytic propellant toward negative thinking and unfulfilling negative action. Happiness and reality easily escape through the slippery portholes of undisciplined anger.

The most frightening answers to this question will come from the most affluent and the most prominent, from the ones closest to you who affect your life. Fear stems from a negative thought producing a negative emotion. This in turn must develop negative brain energy. The answer is without exception, "You Cannot!" It is irrational to support the fantasy that anyone can take a wrong action and get a right result.

It is from the thought within this one sentence that a barrier of human persuasion can be erected. The purpose of this book is to provide through correct information a means to help develop the readers ability to perceive correct information.

"Right Action Requires Right Information."

If it were possible to prove to the reader the reality that the human species is divine, and one, and original, and in itself all-powerful, and that we are truly alike in this reality, then I would be guilty of attempting to prove the impossible.

The purpose of this book is simply to provide, through correct information, the means and method that could allow you-the reader-to empty your mind of those things that are simply not true. Fact, reality and fantasy travel along the same emotional brain circuit, each a separate entity of thought, each needing that separate total sum of the entire emotional brain circuit.

If the mind is not occupied with the emotional energy needed to sustain countless misconceptions, then the reality can be provided to the reader that absolute honesty does indeed invite good luck. This will help provide that tiny opening to the inner circuits of the mind that will permit that small but healing and beneficial intrusion. The rest must be left completely to the opportunities the individual reader is capable of absorbing.

CONFUSION

I would accept the return of my youth only if it were possible to carry back with me the information that has been opened to you, for if I could not, nothing in my life could change toward life's joy that is possible. The same wrong actions based on the same wrong information would merely be replayed.

The information contained in this text is not my original thought, nor does it belong in any way to that person which I am, was, or will be. I have simply re-orchestrated the arrangement for all the instruments. The information must stand by itself, and the reward, pain, freedom, or anguish must be the responsibility of all those wishing to return to that perfection from which we come. This information belongs to all of us. Complicated problems are never resolved; they only tend to confuse and misdirect. The simpler the solution, the more easily the problem becomes open to view, and the more efficiently it is dispensed with.

The information provided from the work must be allowed to stand clear of the flesh to which the author must return again and again. To judge the flesh is to dismiss the spirit. If the writer is judged, the information also becomes judged. The information then could become quite useless and easily dismissed.

ALONE

I'm alone and at times I'm not sure I have even myself. I don't believe I can carry it off. My inner strength is waning from the power of reality and it's deliverance from a debilitating pursuit of a course that seems unnatural. I am drawn in and remain in a safe position. I must hold to deal with what is. I must let the Creator decide what could be. The creation of a new reality from a fantasy must be predicated upon a right concept. This want may become my fading fantasy. I am turning myself to what is and the acceptability of what will be; thus I am excluding the path to pain. I see only the doughnut, not the hole. Looking through the hole, I see too much, and I soon hunger for the doughnut. I'll feed my fat face, then watch television till sleep beckons. I'm a godly vegetable in my own garden. When I'm ripe, I'll pluck myself up and I'll be plucked, my seed left in the ground where a real vegetable might grow. I care of nothing; my vision is turned inward...nothing inward disturbs me. I mirror the world...perhaps God may help us. If there were time! Perhaps the time will be up for me and perhaps that was my vision from the mountain. If that is so, then my son will live to continue.

SELF

To Self: God, why must you be inside of me now to constantly let me know you are there?
Why can you not be in a house of specialty that I could enter and leave of my own choosing?
Why could you not be in the thunderous heavens above, as you once were so mighty and fearfully projected?
Why now must I be reminded that the channel to your seed is where I breathe, where my life thumps, where my heart hungers?
Did you not once reside in a church or other fine and elegant place built for your dominance and perfection?
Why did you leave all those places of splendor to now take permanence in that place within me that is your seed?
Why must you listen to my every thought long after I've forgotten its inner utterance and then play back its melody for me to judge?
Why must I always carry out my own sentence to all the flesh?
Why is my hand moving along this page, and why does each word appear strange and unfamiliar to my mind?
I am glad that it is not I who am writing these words on paper, but only my hand. Or is it my hand?
When my thoughts are not right, my arm pains. When my directions appear wrong, my ankle suddenly aches. When I corrode someone else's reality, my gums rot and my teeth ache. When my thoughts are in conflict with someone else's reality, my head aches. When I rush off in a wrong direction, why am I certain to fall,

or collide with an obvious perceivable reality, or avoid taking a right action, thusly avoiding a right result?
Creator that listens within me! Are we not all geniuses and fools, saints and sinners, givers and takers, virgins and whores, delicates and grubbers, uppers and downers, bleeders and killers, pleasant and difficult, negative and positive, cops and robbers, readers and writers, harmonizers and conflictors? Tell me, am I not the biggest fool of all to imagine that any of this will make a difference? Is this difference for me alone?
In the end, who will protect me?
God will not save me then.
Only the devil will be left, and I shall seek him out. Then I would say to you (if I could, if he would permit), "Stay away, do not listen to me, but know for now you may, you must. But when I look up to God to speak for him, know then that it is time to shut me out."

COMPASSION

Compassion is perhaps mans greatest safety ladder, one of the most self-healing and beneficial of all positive human emotions. It also allows a person-momentarily-a relaxed position away from conflict. It could become helpful in viewing a solution that heretofore was not visible. Unmotivated compassion provides the greatest positive emotional force to developing positive thoughts, increasing natural intelligence, permitting the easy recognition of available correct information. This in turn could develop a right action, which in turn will then provide itself for producing right results. Hence, it will appear that good luck is being invited. On the contrary, the reality is that oncoming bad luck may more readily be avoided.

PERVERSION

Only through Love can sex be Forgiven.......
There are times when through the distorted use of lust, perversions are delivered to invite love, *when it is already present*...The negative result is that it so often replaces love... given time love flows back...But it may not be the same.
Cruel, thoughtless perversion that substitutes for love are not love. (LOVE NEVER HURTS)
More often than not this tends to damage one's natural intelligence, often emptying the mind of positive emotion. This could invite negative brain energy.

SURVIVAL

People who learn to save themselves are persons who are safe to live with. The more people who have accomplished this, the safer you then become. The greater number of safe people that are intermingled with those who aren't, the sturdier the human element in total becomes.

This is not a book based on religious concept, nor does it deal with politics or "isms" of any kind. It cannot be properly described as a form of personal philosophy, but rather it has been inspired to be written by published works of Richard W. Wetherill. The works reflect the absolutes and sanctity of logic; this will then possibly equate itself to your present developing reality. It is the many present projected, distorted, concepts of thoughts (or logic) that have provided the instability now threatening the world. The world I am most referring to specifically, however, is your world, and not necessarily anyone else's. If you become safe through a developing logical mind, it would be proper to accept that you could then project a means of providing to others this most valuable asset. This propensity logically should be pursued without motive. Living within close range of dangerous-thinking, irrational persons, could place your safe position in jeopardy. The premise for actions must always be to save yourself. If you allow yourself to sustain precarious emotional positions of jeopardy, then a personal conclusion soon becomes invited.

I could write on for hundreds of pages on this fascinating conceptual premise, but then I would soon be boring myself, as well as you. The important thrust of the book would never be delivered. I would most certainly lose all but a few fanatical academic geniuses. No matter.

Many human emotional bridges of thought will be provided to view that could deliver an invitation into the acceptance of logic.

THE PROPELLANT OF IT ALL

Why must mans genetic flaw eternally be viewed through the reflection of another? How can one destroy a reflection? Does one need to enter into the mirror of another mans soul to know that he is within himself? Is this not the porthole to hell we too often find ourselves being pushed through? How often do we turn to see who is pushing? How often do we turn to see who is propelling us? How rarely are we able to recognize the face as our own!

When the light is just right-as it is now-it is I that I see.

FANTASY TO REALITY

Man could again live a thousand years or more if he could become absolutely aware of and understand the reality of his genetic flaw.* Man has been burdened with this genetic flaw ever since Adam's rib was rendered for Eve. It is this genetic flaw that will give impetus to a deed that may end us all. The purpose of this book is to deliver a view to this reality that could provide, through correct information, the means that would help to neutralize this negative force.

It is from a view of this often hidden reality that a postponement of that conclusion appears to be possible.

The vehicle I have employed to provide the correct information is this book...

*The genetic flaw is dishonesty.

A THOUGHT

All human change must first come from a thought! The thought that will make the biggest difference must come from you. This book may become instrumental to inviting that important thought that may now be hidden from view. It is this thought to personal right action that could be the means for postponing your final conclusion. There are knowledgeable persons who believe that every person's conclusion has been programmed at conception. This genetic tape for programming defines precisely when one's life has begun to reach its expiration point. Other thoughtful persons accept that through careful exercise of logic, the requirements for taking right actions, this genetically programmed circuit can be bridged. The logic of this conclusion could then help to create a unlimited extension.

ONE...

A person who matters to himself matters to others...
One who hides from oneself is too often hidden from others...
What others should view, never exists...
What never exists should not be seen.
What is not seen is never missed...
What is never missed is never loved...
What is never loved has no life...
What has no life requires no thought.
Perhaps I love you-you are reading my book.
You have thoughts-you do matter to me.
I know you exist-How do you know?
Am I not also you?
Without you...can I exist?
How different we all are!
How we are all so connected!
Are we not all in possession of one...God's original seed?

MY GOD

I am an entity endowed of life from the Creator.
All that is in me is a perfection of his design,
Therefore everything that is in me is God.
I could not be less than what he has endowed me with:
I have his power and his strength only through his thought.
I have none without it.
The thoughts that are left must belong to the devil.
When this is so, as it often is,
The results from my actions confound me.
After the punishment: To repeat and then confess leaves me to address him.-
Only to again accept to repeat...
In the end he will recall me.
Perhaps he will choose to reinstall me.

HELL WITHOUT REALITY

God created all that is reality. His domain remains in the reality around us. The devil must then become the fantasy drawing us away from God's reality. Reality brings us to the protection of the Creator. The distortions of thought predicated from a fantasy allows the presence of the devil, which has been invited. The entity once invited feeds and grows on man's distortions. The devil's advocate seeks and obtains willing recruits. The harmony in hell is in itself a fantasy that soon overwhelms reality. The trap becomes open to all, and all can become subject to its power. The devil appears to give substance to one's life when there seemed to be none. Where man through fantasy was unable to reach God, a voice suggests a number. When dialed, the devil picks up, disconnecting God's line from within...*

* From a letter to Wetherill in early 1979.

SPEAKETH MY SOUL TO CALL HIS NAME

A man hangs from a cliff, too weak to pull himself up to life. As his strength and resolve weaken, he feels himself slipping; he cries from within that silence of his mind where his words have no domain. Yet one word does get through. It is a name, one name that reaches into his spirit and through his conscience. It becomes at once a word cancelling death. His hands become like steel. “God!” he cries.

GETTING GOD TO BELIEVE IN YOU

I do not worship God.
My esteem takes on a higher plane.
One cannot worship an entity and still contain.
The Reality of oneself in relationship to God.
To worship is to expect.
A personal vindication from Man's Genetic Flaw.
Respect and worship develop separate entities of propriety.
To respect is in harmony with reverie.
Worship returns too strongly to self.
There can be no love,-
No reverence,
No harmony without respect.
Respect God rightly
And he will return to you in his purpose
And that is to "Love You."
I cannot speak for him...only through him
As the part of him that resides in me.

IS LOVE A CHALLENGE?

Too many persons have prepared themselves to view and accept love as a challenge. It is from this *negative* perspective that a climate of thought may soon develop that eventually must negate love. A state of mind that invites, heals, and restores love is, of course, that of Acceptance. Eventually the propensity to challenge must soon replace the love.

HOW CAN YOU?

The manifestation from this one thought becomes at once a non-statement, a simplicity of words that perhaps less than one in thirty is capable of understanding and absorbing. It becomes even more rarely understood by persons in position of great power. The sentence is: "Right action brings right results." Without the proper application of the meaning within this one sentence, a person, animal, plant, soon begins to withdraw from the glory of its life. If wrong action is not corrected and eliminated, the terminal time span of all life becomes withdrawn.

The statement that "Right Action Brings Right Result's," has a corollary: "One cannot take a wrong Action and get a right result," regardless of the situation or the extent of one's faith or hope. Were you to ask numerous people, "Is it possible to get a right result by taking a wrong action?", The answers would at first amuse, then concern you, then perhaps frighten you, and then convince you. Can you take a wrong action and get a right result? How can you? If you attained a right result it would simply indicate that you had taken a right action. It would be illogical to assume otherwise.

DECISION MAKERS VERSES RULES

Rules of all sorts for all reasons are put in place to remove responsibility for the Decision-maker. Thus the decision-maker cannot make a decision without putting a rule in place.

For this, he or she would need a consensus for installing a rule that would absolve him or her of all responsibility.
In prisons, generally, no independent decision can be made without adhering to a rule. To do so would invariably lead to punishment. This punishment is another rule. The rule may or may not seem fair. There is little redress for the punishment. The prisoner is always deemed guilty of the broken rule no matter what.

The continuous mode for enforcement is fear. The Judge and Jury is usually the guard, warden or the psychologist....
In most cases, should the prisoner protest, the punishment is even more severe. He has lost all independent and or personal thought to action. In order to survive in most prisons, the prisoner must become mindless. **FEAR IS ALWAYS THE CONTROL!**

Rarely is human compassion shown to the troublesome prisoner. When non-is given, and the prisoner is treated like an animal, his reactions must become bitter.

FEAR IS THE UNDERPINNING OF HATE...

TRAGEDY PROTECTION

The greatest protection a human being can avail himself of is his ability to view, accept, and exercise logic, without which he will come to fantasize and then blunder so as to meet his genetically programmed timetable marking the time for his likely conclusion. This is so ordained, not only by the genetic tapes inherited from his parents, but to some larger degree by reactions from his environmental nest-the air he breathes and the circumstances in which he allows himself to develop from his thought. He is most often forced to follow a prescribed pattern of thinking dedicated from emotional patterns. The purpose of this work is to open, to view in the least obtrusive and most inviting manner the means to rearrange these orders of things into words that could lead to the most realistic progressions of thought. The solutions offered may appear to be simple, but accepting them will not be easy.

LOVE NEEDS NO AFFIRMATION

Pleasure needs to be too often repeated and proven (for example, sex, drinking, smoking, eating, drugs...). love needs no such affirmation. When it flows, it is as if by magic. It cannot be controllable. If treated with respect and compassion, acceptance and affection, and held in decent reverence, love continues. It then becomes sturdy enough to overcome all negative emotions. It can become vulnerable and quite fragile through substantial distorted judgments. It can continue endlessly, tirelessly, healing, nourishing, growing, multiplying, until it is finally murdered properly by a "Yes U-Can"; but given enough time it will rise somewhere else again. Again perhaps to be murdered. Someone somewhere must shout to the assassins: "STOP U-CANNOT!"

FOCUS

The parables along with the Klooog stories will be a source to provide creditability to the answers from the Reality Quiz. Some of the answers that will be revealed to you through this search should electrify your thinking. Your freshly reawakened thinking prowess will amaze you. The profundity of joyful knowledge that will clear the clogged circuits of your thinking process will have your mind smiling at your weakened distortions, releasing many painful confusing misconceptions that heretofore may have been preventing you from reaching your full mental potential efficiency.

A VERY PERSONAL TEST THAT MAY HELP YOU TO ACHIEVE YOUR FULL POTENTIAL MENTAL EFFICIENCY

This is a test designed to measure not your academic ability or your knowledge of facts and figures, but rather to measure your ability to use your natural mental energy to its highest potential. The test will help provide a new approach as to how you may best view and overcome some of your negative inhibitions. It will also provide a means for you to focus your thoughts to solutions heretofore not open to personal view because of personal problems that may be preventing you from achieving all the success due you.

If you are able to achieve a perfect score of 100 %-you are functioning at your full potential mental efficiency. Attaining a score of 80 % or thirty two correct answers is a strong indication that you are functioning at 80 % of your natural mental potential. There is room for improvement. However, the score is excellent, indicating that you may be borderline to genius. Attaining a score of twenty correct answers, or 50 %, is quite good, indicating that you are probably functioning at 50 % of your natural potential. This is a clear indication that there is room for improvement. This could be your key to self-fulfillment. More importantly, you should be aware of this.

If you have a score of 25 % or less, this book could mean more to you than any words of mine could describe.

BEFORE TAKING THE REALITY QUIZ

1. Would you like to know how really intelligent you still are?

2. Are you aware of how much intelligence you may have lost as you have acquired knowledge through education and from life's experience?

3. Do you consider yourself to be a logical person?

4. How logically safe are you under stressful situations?

5. How often have you been able to deliver yourself to a logical decision under the difficulties brought about by conflicts of developing stress?

The Reality Quiz is designed to provide an access that could help to reinstall your full potential mental efficiency. More than fifty years study and meticulous research has developed credibility to the information from which this Reality Quiz has been structured.

REALITY STATEMENTS: ARE THEY TRUE OR FALSE? (A TEST TO MEASURE YOUR CAPACITY TO VIEW LOGIC)

There are forty statements, all to be either answered True or False. You may take as much time as you require. However, truthful answers are usually those that come to us most readily and represent the thinking we are accustomed to being guided by in our daily life. The correct answers are given on the final page of this book.

	TRUE	FALSE
1. Love and sex are two absolutely separate entities.	______	______
2. Pornography can damage and diminish natural intelligence.	______	______
3. Love is a state of mind devoid of judgment.	______	______
4. Truth and facts rarely correspond to reality.	______	______
5. Placing oneself into positions that require trust may soon develop into acts of absolute immorality.	______	______
6. A wrong action does not always produce a wrong result.	______	______

	TRUE	FALSE
7. Positioning information to judgment renders the information useless.	______	______
8. A right action must produce a sustained right result.	______	______
9. A right result can follow a wrong action.	______	______
10. The degree of trust and faith one develops is related to one's ability to view reality.	______	______
11. Dishonesty sometimes invites bad luck.	______	______
12. Absolute honesty increases natural intelligence.	______	______
13. Brain energy develops only from emotion.	______	______
14. Right action can be taken with wrong information.	______	______
15. Brain energy is not required to sustain a misconception.	______	______
16. All unhappiness comes from wants.	______	______

	TRUE	FALSE
17. Good luck develops from perceiving correct information.	______	______
18. Some lies are a distortion.	______	______
19. Every distortion is a lie.	______	______
20. Excessive viewing of television seduces the mind to invite instant pleasure.	______	______
21. Gambling is a form of competition.	______	______
22. Competition develops conflict.	______	______
23. Stress has no effect on intelligence.	______	______
24. Harmony blocks stress.	______	______
25. Stress does not block reality.	______	______
26. Confusion develops insecurity.	______	______
27. Correct information allows right actions.	______	______
28. Blocking reality develops fantasy.	______	______
29. Fantasy vacates reality.	______	______

	TRUE	FALSE
30. Right action does not require right intent.	______	______
31. Motives replace right intent.	______	______
32. Absolute honesty vacates wrong intent.	______	______
33. Wrong thought invites wrong action.	______	______
34. Fantasy and reality share the same mental circuit.	______	______
35. Logic blocks negative thoughts.	______	______
36. Wants grow in fantasy.	______	______
37. Fantasy substitutes happiness.	______	______
38. Right action fortifies logic.	______	______
39. Judgments replace information.	______	______
40. Good luck reflects one's ability to perceive correct information.	______	______